Your Amazing Itty Bitty™ Grief to Grace Book

15 Key Steps to Transforming the Sadness of Loss to Joy

Sherry Shoemaker, PhD

Published by Itty Bitty™ Publishing
A subsidiary of S & P Productions, Inc.

Printed in the United States of America

Itty Bitty Publishing
311 Main Street, Suite D
El Segundo, CA 90245
(310) 640-8885

ISBN: 978-1-959964-79-7

This book is for educational purposes only. Nothing should be taken as mental health advice, diagnosis or treatment. Always seek the guidance of a mental health professional should you need assistance.

Your Amazing Itty Bitty™ Grief to Grace Book

15 Key Steps to Transforming the Sadness of Loss into Joy

Grief is a journey of the heart and one you don't have to take alone. Whether it's the loss of a home to fire, a job, a loved one, a pet, a relationship or even a sense of identity, grief can leave you feeling lost, overwhelmed and unsure how to move forward. The grief that ensues can be devastating. It is an emotional experience, not a mental one. Most people don't know how to grieve or even know it is okay to do so. Society doesn't give you the tools, or many times the space, to feel your feelings, or the ability to process what you are feeling.

In *Your Amazing Itty Bitty™ Grief to Grace Book*, Dr. Sherry Shoemaker gently gives you direction and practical steps to bring you to your best, joy-filled life, while honoring your loved ones, yourself and your life situation.

Inside, you'll discover how to:

- Embrace vulnerability as a strength
- Find grace and meaning in mourning
- Identify healthy, supportive connections
- Build emotional resilience
- And so much more

If you or someone you love is facing loss, pick up your copy of this Itty Bitty™ book today and take the first step from grief to grace.

Dedication

To my Beautiful Daughter, Diane
1987-2023

Stop by our Itty Bitty™ website to find interesting blog entries regarding Grief to Grace.

www.IttyBittyPublishing.com

Or visit Dr. Sherry Shoemaker, PhD, at

https://www.askdrsherryusa.com
askdrsherryusa@gmail.com
760-291-7792

Table of Contents

Introduction

From grief to grace.

Everyone has had a loss in their life. It can be anything from moving and disconnection from friends to divorce, losing a job you love, losing a beloved pet, losing a spouse, child, partner, family member—anyone or anything you are close to and identify with.

Grief is an emotional process, not a mental one. But how many people know what grief is or how to grieve in a healthy way? Overall, our society doesn't give you the tools, or many times space to feel your feelings, and the ability to process what you're feeling.

This book gives you a direction and practical steps to bring you to your best joy-filled life while honoring your loved one, yourself and your life situation.

The principles in this book are *universal* truths. The steps are relevant and simple (note I didn't say always easy). Yes, you have to *change* the inertia of sadness to the glow of participating in life.

I know because I practiced these steps and still do, as I go through life after the most profound loss of my life: the unexpected death of my 35-year-old daughter.

So, let the adventure begin!

Step 1
The Landscape of Grief

Grief is considered sad and unhappy. It's an emotion that goes across the spectrum from mildly annoying and creating a glitch in your everyday life, to debilitating, where you can't get out of bed at all, overwhelmed, stuck, gray and numb.

1. Grief is unexpected. It totally changes your life.
2. Grief is chaotic, debilitating and over-whelming.
3. Grief takes you totally by surprise and knocks you flat.

Grief can take many forms: the loss of a home, a divorce, losing a job, losing a child, partner, spouse, parent, pet and even a lifestyle.

1. All of these create a grieving process you need to acknowledge and allow.
2. The process is not linear. It doesn't go from A to Z.
3. Processing the emotions of grief isn't tidy; it's messy.

More About the Landscape of Grief

Grief is not a destination. It's a moment to take stock of who and where you are.

- Allow this time to be with yourself.
- Allow your feelings, even though they are uncomfortable and inconvenient.
- Be kind to yourself.
- Give yourself grace.
- Trust your instincts.
- The landscape of loss is yours alone to navigate.
- Your grief will transform, just like nature does from winter to summer.

Your grief isn't static. Grief weaves itself into your life. The relationship with your loss changes; moments of joy become more abundant, like a bouquet of favorite flowers.

Step 2
Deconstructing the Myth of Loss to Challenge Hopelessness

A myth is a story or symbolic narrative of un-known origin. Many are raised to think of loss as sad and hopeless, without seeing the opportunity and lesson inside the story.

1. You learn how to feel about loss and grief from church, parents and cultural traditions.
2. You are taught from an early age not to challenge traditions or cultural rules.
3. For every action there is a reaction (scientific principle).
4. For every negative thought, there is a positive thought (the law of the universe). Change is inevitable. Growth is optional.

Every loss creates a grieving process. The challenge is whether you let it define you or use it to create an opportunity.

1. Cry, be sad and allow yourself to go through your emotions.
2. Choose whether you want to withdraw or live fully.
3. Challenge the old myth and create your own reality.

More on the Myth of Loss

Loss happens to everyone, and everyone reacts to loss differently. A modern myth wants everyone to be the same as a way to promote and predict unity in thoughts and actions without questioning the history of the tradition.

- Don't let anyone tell you how to grieve.
- Real harmony comes from understanding and embracing differences.
- Allow yourself to follow your heart.

Uniqueness is part of being human. It is not a flaw; it's a strength. Remember you are valuable, capable and amazing.

Sameness can be a source of control, pressure to do what your family has done before. Challenge the prevalent idea of failure and hopelessness. Look for your lesson; be the new you. Embrace the messy variety of your human experience. See LOVE in the void your loss created.

Step 3
Where Spirit Takes You:
Navigating Storms and Calming Your Inner World

Your loss has occurred. Your grief is profound. One minute you're crying, the next you're angry, and the next exhausted. You might laugh at a memory, then criticize yourself for a moment of happiness.

1. You are human.
2. Emotions in mourning are fluid.
3. Dr. Elizabeth Kubler-Ross defined five stages of grieving: denial, anger, bargaining, depression and acceptance. The stages do not go in linear order. Give yourself time; there will be a new normal.

You might have been taught to suppress emotions, to only express them in private, or that throwing a tantrum will achieve what you want. Neither extreme is the answer.

1. Grieving is a process, and allowing yourself to feel is normal.
2. It is okay to ask for positive, healthy support.
3. Grieving is messy.

More About Where Spirit Takes You

Spirit, God, intuition, inner guidance, whatever you call it, is a very important part of you. It guides you to make decisions that are right for you, but you have to *listen.*

- The real inner you never tells you to do something hurtful to yourself or others.
- Your inner you loves you.
- Take time to really listen.
- The outside world doesn't always have your best interests at heart.
- It can seem like help is everywhere and nowhere.
- You decide what is best for you.

Step 4
Grace in Mourning:
Give Yourself a Gentle Break!

You grieve in your own way! The average length of time to grieve is about a year, 12 months. When it continues for more than three years, it is called prolonged grief disorder. It's not necessary to go to that extreme. Remember, you have only one life to live. Live is the operative word.

1. Remember, this is your experience. It may be the first time for you. Even if it isn't, every time is different.
2. Allow yourself time. Grieving is not a race to get back to normal.
3. You have a new normal now. This is a time to look around you and make new decisions to go forward.

Give yourself the grace of time, where thought and observation are not a luxury but a necessity.

1. Go with the process.
2. Trying to hold it together and be strong only makes everything take longer.
3. Listen to yourself, to the inner voice that only has your highest good in mind.

More About Giving Yourself Grace

You're taught to be responsible, to get back to whatever you were doing before, and do it the same or better. You learned to resist asking for help. Your mantra has always been, "I can do it myself."

- Grief is messy; if you don't try to tie it up in a neat package, the journey/process will be smoother.
- You are the most important person in this moment. BE KIND TO YOURSELF!
- Just like in an airplane, put on your own oxygen mask first.

Be the easy effortless, flowing water between two rocks. Breathe, dance; physical movement enhances oxygen flow, cell rejuvenation and blood flow.

Step 5
Re-identify Yourself:
Who Are You Now?

Before your loss, you were the boss, the parent, the child, the owner, the … you name it! Now you're not. Everything about you has changed. Now is the time to learn more about *you*.

1. Think about yourself in a new way.
2. Ask yourself questions, such as: What do you like? And what are your strengths?
3. How can you develop interests from the past into new opportunities?

Family, friends and coworkers may not realize how your world has changed and that you need time for yourself. They may encourage you to do what you've always done and stop being dramatic or sorry for yourself.

1. No one knows what you're going through, unless you tell them.
2. If they don't want to hear it, you don't need them around you right now.
3. Tell them nicely that you'll contact them when you're ready.

More About How to Re-identify Yourself

To re-identify yourself, you must take a journey, and like every journey, sometimes it's not a straight line from start to finish.

- You can change your mind about who you are.
- You can try different things.
- Everything is new for you now, and it may take a few tries to feel comfortable moving forward.
- No judgment or criticism is allowed.
- Have fun with this part of the process.
- Laugh and enjoy yourself.
- Be your own beta tester.
- Since there is no such thing as perfect, get out of your old comfort zone.
- Do nothing and be everything.

Step 6
Future Life Story:
Five Steps to Being You

You may be asking where to begin. Here are five ways for you to get started. Remember, no judgment about what you want and no inner critic about how to get there.

1. Start journaling every day.
2. Use the words love and gratitude at least once in your journal every day.
3. Mind map your future. Draw a circle on paper and write your name on it. Draw sun rays and write a few words to describe your future self.
4. Start with the word loving.
5. Use as many words as you want.

Your future may seem bleak at first and not fun. You are a living, breathing, valuable human, worthy of a vibrant life.

1. You may start feeling sad. That's okay. Keep writing and use the words love and gratitude. You'll feel the change over time, sooner rather than later.
2. You are precious.
3. Your loss does not define you.

More About Your Future Life

As you write and imagine what you want, your future life gradually becomes your present life. It's amazing how change occurs easily and effortlessly when you take simple actions every day.

- Add color and pictures/drawings to your journal.
- Write silly, ridiculous things that make you laugh. Add humor and laughter to your life with one new physical activity every day.
- Watch funny videos and laugh out loud.
- Go for a walk, run or skip.
- See yourself in a race, at the gym or in a dance studio. Go, go, go; just do it!

Step 7
Embracing Vulnerability:
Emotions = Superpower

When you're grieving, just going through the process makes you feel vulnerable and out of control. You don't have all the answers like you usually do. What else can happen? Life is suddenly scary with chaos.

1. New emotions come to the forefront during the grieving process.
2. Fear, lack, failure, anxiety and confusion can crowd in on you.

Every time you acknowledge an emotion that makes you feel vulnerable or out of control, counter it with a powerful emotion that gives you strength and confidence.

1. Words are important. They carry a frequency that shapes how you live your life.
2. Confidence, abundance, success, calm and peace are all high-frequency words and emotions.

More About Embracing Vulnerability

Being vulnerable is defined as opening yourself to risk, rejection, hurt or potential harm. The superpower of opening yourself to others is the ability to see new pieces of yourself that may not have been acceptable in your previous relationship, job, neighborhood or lifestyle.

- Step out more as yourself: strong and happy.
- Define your superpowers and write them out.
- Make a point of living those powers daily.
- No more keeping up appearances for the sake of appearances.
- No more people pleasing; please yourself instead.

Give yourself permission to feel. There's no "right way" to grieve, and your emotions are valid.

Find safe spaces to open up—whether it's with trusted people, in a journal or with a therapist or a coach.

Accept that healing isn't linear. Feeling exposed one day and composed the next is normal.

Step 8
Healthy Support:
Boundaries Mark Your Territory!

When you have a loss and you're grieving, people will offer to help you. What they don't say is they want to help you *their way,* which makes it easier for them to be around you. Your life has changed. You are in the midst of change. Not everyone understands that!

1. Your friends want to take you out with them because it's "best for you" not to mope around.
2. They're not listening.
3. Your boss wants you back at work and keeps calling you with work questions.
4. Your family wants to know what you're doing next and when!

You're in crisis, and the people you thought you could count on, just want more and more from you.

1. Why can't you suck it up and get on with your life?
2. When will you decide about the trip we planned before your loss?
3. All you need is a two-day retreat, and you'll be all better.

More About Healthy Support

This is the time when you decide what is best for you now. You don't want to be rude or appear to be unappreciative, but this is not the time to be people-pleasing. You need this time to become the new person you are. Renew friendships and relations from your new perspective, not the old one.

- You can nicely say, "Thank you. Let me call you when I'm ready."
- You do not have to explain yourself.
- You do not have to answer questions that make you uncomfortable.
- You do not have to allow family to over-whelm you with their ideas of what is right for you.
- You choose what is right for you.
- Setting boundaries for your health and well-being is your right.
- Boundary-setting is healthy, not selfish.

Brene Brown's qualitative research (e.g., from her book *Daring Greatly)* shows that people with the strongest sense of compassion and empathy are those who set clear, firm boundaries. Boundaries protect energy and prevent resentment. Self-care often involves setting boundaries—not to exclude others, but to preserve your capacity to connect authentically.

Step 9
Honor Legacy:
A Weight or a Gift

In the case of a loved one's death, you may have a way to remember them. You might have written instructions about how to honor a legacy through a trust or a will. You might create your own way to do it. The legacy is generally something that your loved one wants to be known for when you think of them.

1. You smile when you think of them.
2. You remember fun events filled with laughter.
3. Your heart opens with love when you think of them.

There are many ways to honor a legacy. Many have to do with rebirth, love and growth.

1. Buy a plant and nurture it.
2. Create a drawing of something that reminds you of them.
3. Enjoy an activity you did together.

More About Honoring Legacy

Think and feel into what your loved one would want for you. Would they want misery and loneliness? Or for you to be happy living a full joy-filled life?

- Do you want your grief to be a weight on your life and heart?
- Do you want grief to be a gift with a sparkle in your eye and love in your heart?
- You get to choose. Those choices are yours to make.
- Honoring a loved one's legacy isn't about perfect tribute—it's about connection, healing and meaning. Whether quiet and private or shared and visible, your remembrance can be as unique as the person you lost.
- Rituals give structure to mourning and help externalize emotional expression.
- According to grief expert Robert Neimeyer, meaning-making is essential to adapting to loss. Honoring a loved one can help people integrate their loss into their life story (Neimeyer, 2001).

Step 10
See Love, Express Love:
Explore Your Emotional Connections

Maybe you never thought about it, but you have emotional connections with the people in your family, the neighbors, the guy who fixes your car, the bully at work and the loss you're grieving. Some emotions are deeper than others, but put them all together and you're exhausted by them.

1. You do not have to engage with any of the emotional connections.
2. A negative emotion is not worth your energy.
3. Take care of yourself first when around people who only want to take from you.

It takes effort on your part. Go into connections with a feeling of peace and love, and a feeling that things are different now.

1. Show up smiling.
2. Before you connect with anyone, play the meeting in your head to rehearse how you want it to go.
3. Keep in mind that being happy and expressing love honors you and your loved one's legacy. That's your goal.

More About Seeing and Expressing Love

It's hard to think loving thoughts and see others in a loving way when previous experience wasn't the best.

- You are developing new habits.
- It gets easier every time you practice.
- It will seem like a sudden shift to the other person, because YOU have already made the change.
- You will not be emotionally triggered by the same behaviors anymore.

The result is you're a more loving, happier person to yourself and life is brighter.

Love After Loss Can Be Found In:

Memory	Feeling warmth from a shared moment or phrase
People	Friends/family who offer support or just sit in silence
Nature	Feeling connected while watching a sunset or walking in solitude
Spirituality	Sensing the presence of the loved one or divine love
Acts of Kindness	Receiving or giving empathy, generosity or patience

Step 11
Vibrant Life After Loss:
Strategies to Embody Joy and Purpose

You rarely see loss, grieving and joy, love and purpose in the same sentence. They are at two ends of the emotional spectrum. You could say they're two sides of the same coin.

1. You want to live vibrantly, full of joy and purpose, because that's what you're here for.
2. All of it takes practice.
3. You may not know the feeling of joy.
4. You may not know what to call your purpose.

The strategy for living life with joy and purpose is as follows.

1. Don't worry about it!
2. Laugh every day several times; even at silly things that used to be annoying, laugh at all of it.
3. Only do things you love. If someone asks you, for example, why you're digging that hole, say out loud, "Because I love doing it."
4. If you don't love doing something, Just Say No! and don't do it.

More About Strategies for a Vibrant Life After Loss

You are moving on an upward path from the depths where loss and grieving can take you. Be patient and consistent. Love yourself first.

- Get that journal out! Write all the bright, lovely things you saw in the last 12 hours. You can write the same thing for days at a time. Describe the colors. Draw pictures of them.
- Dance every morning before you leave the house.
- Dance every evening before you go to bed.
- Do something new, your choice.
- Have an adventure. Build a tent in your living room and sleep in it.
- Volunteer somewhere you love for as much time as you're comfortable with.

Step 12
Emotional Resilience:
Activating Your Strength With Experience

You just don't realize how strong you can be, like a mother lifting a car to free her child. You lose sight of what you've accomplished in life—what you've gone through and survived. When an unexpected loss occurs, it fills your mind and everything else falls out!

1. Now is the time to remember how you got through the last emotional crisis.
2. Write down the top three events in your life that affected you deeply at the time. This doesn't have to be a loss.
3. Take those moments, remember the feeling of getting through it, and the strength you felt.

Resilience is facing those same feelings. Maybe the situation changes, but the *feelings* are there and moving through the scary negative side to a successful, happy ending every time.

1. Every time is a new time.
2. The more experience, the better you are at recognizing and getting through the tough spots.
3. Celebrate! You are awesome.

More About Emotional Resilience

Do you have high emotional resilience? How do you come back from tough circumstances? If you have high emotional resilience, setbacks only set you back for a short time. You move forward with determination and clarity.

- A loss, including a death, is a lesson to be learned.
- You look for ways to move forward and continue living.

To build emotional resilience, take your moments of sadness and acknowledge them. Create new habits, such as the following.

- Set realistic goals for yourself.
- Focus on self-compassion.
- Develop a supportive network of friends and family to listen and embrace what you choose to do.
- Get daily physical exercise.
- Write in your journal every day.

Step 13
Continuous Love:
Maintaining Meaningful Relationships

Grief and love are deeply intertwined in loss. Jaime Anderson, author of *Dr. Who,* wrote, "Grief is love with nowhere to go." It's up to you to create a new path for the love you feel. Find a way to honor your connection with the person or event as you adapt to the feeling of absence. When you want to maintain relationships, you simultaneously process pain while trying to remain present for others.

1. You experience a "new normal" with your relationships.
2. Love and honor have new meaning for you.
3. Be selective about who you reach out to for support.

Recognize your need for connection in a new way. Allow yourself to redefine and clarify what you want.

1. Explain your new normal, and explain again as your needs evolve.
2. Allow others to respond their way, then you can choose what and who is right for you.

More About Continuous Love

There are practical approaches to maintaining relationships while grieving. When you're ready to make healthy changes that work for you, look at these options.

- Create grief-inclusive spaces: integrate your grief into relationships instead of compartmentalizing. Don't hesitate to bring up the subject and allow your emotions.
- Find balance: alternate between grief-focused time and connection-focused time. You need both to move forward in a healthy way.

What makes relationships meaningful isn't just support and function but how they help you continue loving a person, a pet, an event you lost, and the people still in your life.

- Nurture flexible expectations
- Grow together with the important people in your life
- Foster meaningful relationships more than ever before

Step 14
Rituals and Remembrances:
Creative Ways to Process Loss and
Honor Legacy

Rituals and remembrances are frameworks to honor connections with those you've lost. Loss is about death of a loved one, family or pet. These rituals are part of the grief process and help transform absence into living memories.

1. Many cultures and religions have rituals to help remember family and pets.
2. You can create your own memory and how you want to honor your loved one.
3. The ritual can change over time with no regrets.

Create your own memories, such as the following:

1. Repurpose clothing by creating a memory quilt.
2. Learn a skill or craft they practiced and form a living connection through skill inheritance.

More About Rituals and Remembrances

Holding onto a place or situation doesn't help. It can stop you from healing and appreciating new people and opportunities as follows:

- You're processing the loss of a house, job, relationship or other life-altering event.
- You're proud to get a paycheck, even though you complained about your boss or coworkers every day.
- You feel sad because now you're going to events alone without your spouse or partner due to divorce.
- You think you'll never get a better house, even though you didn't like the view, the patio or the plants that never grew where you previously lived.

Step 15
Happy Grief™ Practices:
A Summary

Happy Grief™ is another way of saying, "I am living fully with joy and grace. I understand the grieving process and its main stages: denial, anger, bargaining, depression and acceptance."

1. As you go through the stages in the usual messy way of all grieving people, you find memories to smile about.
2. You start activities to expand the life that shrank when you faced an unexpected loss.
3. You know that acceptance is not forgetting, but instead remembering in a way that is a gift, not a weight.

Everyone grieves differently, and each loss has its own impact level on you. So, it's important for you to take care of yourself first.

1. Taking care of yourself first gives you the ability to be kind to others who are going through the same loss.
2. You understand yourself without judgment or criticism.
3. Your story is not the same as other families or friends.
4. You are made for love and life.

More About Happy Grief™ Practices

Scientists say that it takes 30 to 60 days to change a habit, including how you think about things. That means consistent practice for 30-60 days. *Make it something you do every day, or start counting over again.*

Start with just one thing.

- Journal, include drawings and colors.
- Include the words: gratitude and love in your journal every day.
- What do you love today?
- What are you grateful for?
- In your first week of journaling, start walking 2,500 steps every day. If you can do it at the same time every day, all the better.
- Take naps when you're tired. Start right away.
- Be kind to yourself; cry when you want to.
- Grief to grace, to Happy Grief ™ is a process.

To know more about the process, go to https://www.askdrsherryusa.com and schedule a grief assessment call.

You've finished. Before you go…

Post/Share that you finished this book.

Please star rate this book.

Reviews are solid gold to writers. Please take a few minutes to give us some itty bitty feedback.

ABOUT THE AUTHOR

Dr. Sherry Shoemaker, PhD, MTOM, RN, brings over 40 years of experience in the medical field, with a rich background as a registered nurse and acupuncturist. For 20 years, she has provided compassionate care as an acupuncturist, helping individuals manage their physical and emotional well-being. Throughout her career, Dr. Shoemaker has navigated many challenging experiences, including witnessing both expected and unexpected deaths while supporting families in the hospital setting.

Her personal journey took an unexpected turn with the death of her daughter, a profound loss that deeply shaped her understanding of grief. Through her own grieving process, Dr. Shoemaker developed the revolutionary concept of "Happy Grief," a transformative approach that challenges the conventional view of loss as solely a source of sadness and hopelessness.

Learn more and contact Dr. Sherry Shoemaker by going to: https://www.askdrsherryusa.com.

If you enjoyed this Itty Bitty™ book, you might also like…

Your Amazing Itty™ Stress Reduction Book - Denise Thompson

Your Amazing Itty Bitty™ Grief Book - Lisa Herrington

Your Amazing Itty Bitty™ Conscious Co-Creation Book - Heidi Katara Funk

Or any of the many Amazing Itty Bitty™ books available online at www.ittybittypublishing.com.